Circadia

Alison Watt

To Leah,
Alison Watt

Pedlar Press | Toronto

ACKNOWLEDGEMENTS

The publisher wishes to thank the Canada Council for the Arts and the Ontario Arts Council for their generous support of our publishing program.

LIBRARY AND ARCHIVES CANADA CATALOGUING IN PUBLICATION DATA

Watt, Alison, 1957-
Circadia / Alison Watt.
Poems.

ISBN 1-897141-02-5

I. Title.
PS8645.A87C57 2005 C811'.6 C2005-903718-0

First Edition

COVER Alison Watt, *Red Study*, 2004

DESIGN Zab Design & Typography, Winnipeg

Printed in Canada

For Lindsay and Sophie

Contents

Thesis

The Distance

Circadia

Kingdom of Chlorophyll

Thesis

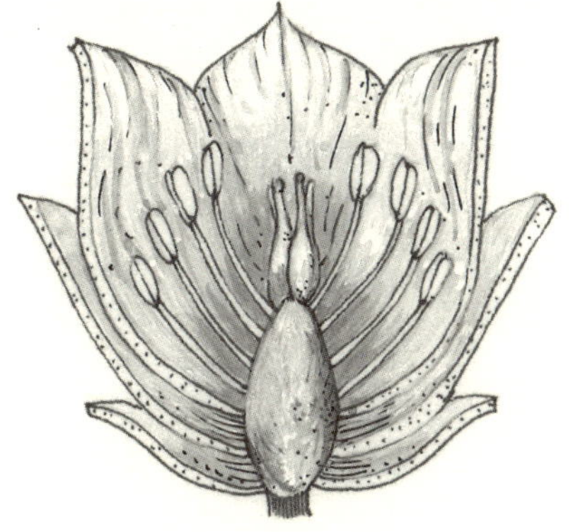

Pine Island

If the wind had been up
if the tides were running,
you might have decided that crossing
wasn't worth the risk.

I could've taken a break
from studying nesting gulls,
accepted an invitation
to go out fishing on a passing troller.

Even after you crossed ten miles of open water
hunched over the outboard of a rental boat at dusk
just to cook me dinner,
we could have gone on
almost strangers.

I might not have found you
in the city at the end of summer.

You could have married a linguist from Sweden,
had seven blue-eyed children.

It might not have happened like this:
you brought a bottle of Beaujolais
saw a secret mole on my left hip
your skin smelled like salt and gasoline.

The Botanist's Lover

We leave the sidewalk's dead language
of crabgrass and plantain.

Even in remnant forest
night is fluent:
deer fern, salal, snowberry.

I gather Latin roots,
vowels slipped from stems.

For now I call the arc of you
"Monotropa uniflora"—ghost plant
pale limbs rising from the earth,
smelling of pine needles.

Above us leaves exhale,
rain moves through veins.

My fingers trace articulations,
a meadow ripens in my mouth.
A new taxonomy
to know and name you.

Thesis

I spend my days in the herbarium.

In cool chambers
the specimens lie, pressed
and opened by botanists' gentle hands.

Below the tall windows
caned by rain
I sift through brittle blooms.

Years have passed since moth wings stirred their petals.

I'm unmoved
by the rattle of their dry pods,
chromosomes clenched in unsown seed.

Small embryo,
the night you planted yourself
in the dark of my belly
you became my only thesis.

I'll record the curve of your scapula,
measure the days and nights until your birth,
weigh this suspended love.

Under my heart
already you're reaching for the light,
budding white fists, petalled fingers.

Maternity Ward — St. Paul's

Blood on the sheets.
The sharp cries of my son
hook in my breasts and belly.

I dream of the Sisters of Providence
nurses who slept in these rooms
at the top of the hospital.

When I surface from sleep
I'm smooth and chambered,
solitary as a nautilus.

He's here, mysterious creature
smelling of ocean,
eyes wide open, surprised
by the unholy light,
the sudden weight of air.

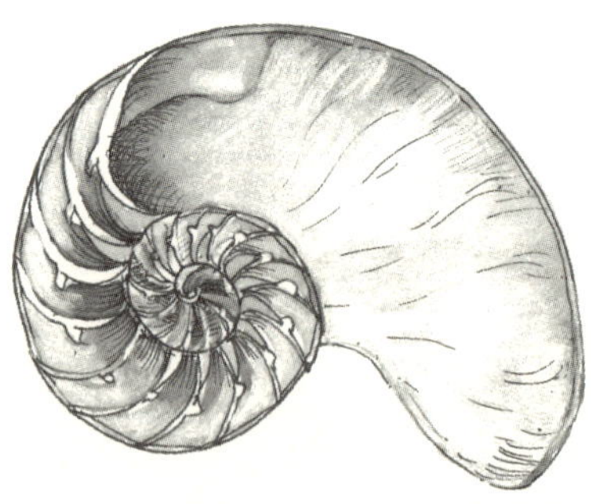

Summer River

I take my small son to the river
where the narrow glance of sky opens
and the water slows
in its long flex through sandstone.

The river has lost the smell of snow,
trawls sap and earth,
the liquid breath of fish.

He stands on the bank
watching the water slide through spindled light.

Under sunken ledges
stone-coloured trout hang
as cool and unblinking
as the grown boys
(who dive too shallow, swim too deep)
pulled from the river each summer.

My son brings his elbows to his ribs.
The green stare must be broken—
he laughs and jumps,
pale body rippling like a lure.

Spring Eclipse

Tonight, while the earth drags
its umbral hand over the moon's cold Braille,
you're asleep in your small beds,
the first frogs are singing
and we can't go out to find them among the lily stalks.

I want to tell you
that when the moon was new
no waters lay below it,
that as the earth began to cool
the rain fell and filled the hollows;
about the gathering of fire
in green alder leaf;
the smouldering in our cells, consuming stars.

I want to tell you
while you sleep
a million helices unspool
their ciphered tongues in the night,
filling the bottomless ponds of your dreams
with frog song,
filling the world with strange fruit.

T. rex — Tyrrell Museum

A month after the accident
I push my daughter in a wheelchair—
her leg is mending
in its own sweet time.

We stroll past dinosaurs
posed in the moment of predation
until we find the one she's looking for,
a skeleton rising to the vault.

She stares up at its scaffold of ribs,
wrecking ball and socket, the seized
machinery of teeth.

I want to take her outside
where we can listen to meadowlarks.

What can we unearth here
but an endless reassembling of bones,
stripped of flesh and song
no matter how fierce.

Sonogram

The woman in the garden is the one listening.
In her memory they'll be joined:
boy at the piano,
finch in the fir crown.

All the boy knows are notes
flying from his fingers.

The bird doesn't hear what's not important:
wind, a siren,
how the boy summons everything
for difficult passages.

For days the finch has sung from tree to tree,
staking place. Vigilant,
he only hears the next finch over—
much must be defended
in this short season.

The boy won't notice
the bird fallen silent—
he'll have loaded the trunk of the Corolla
with winter clothes, urtext sonatas,
be gone before migration.

The woman will be left,
thinking of territories
begun to grow over.

Unconceived

Tonight I hear you crying.
You are a baby seal
I rescue from the mouth of a dog.

I try to hold you
but you struggle out of my arms.

For years I saved a space for you,
felt you were waiting
for me to decide.

A plan so simple
I could do it in my sleep. I didn't notice
time running out

until the day last spring
when I threw your grandmother's ashes into the sea.

You were to inherit
her easy laugh,
a space between your front teeth,
the dark hair and green eyes
the others never got.

All day high tides drown the rocks.
My reflection in the window, a face
beginning to wear its age.
I feel your passing—
a selkie, shedding human shape.

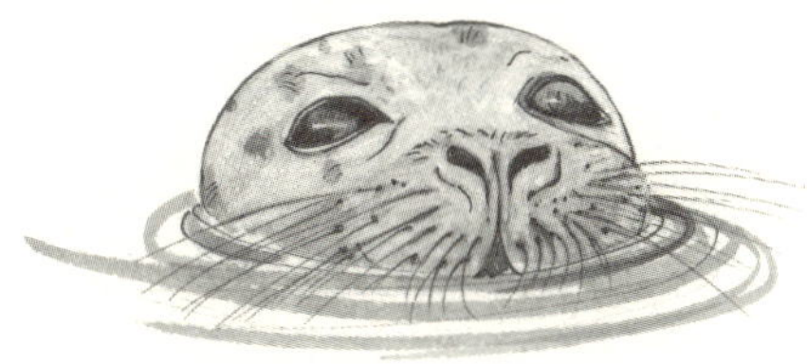

Highway

Driving to your piano lesson,
I watch the roadside for flickers and red-tailed hawks.
We cross the intersection
where your friend's father died one rainy night not long ago.
Wilted flowers are taped to the metal light posts.
I ask, "How's Tom?"
You shrug. "He seems fine."
At twelve, you don't notice,
can't guess how each moment carries you forward.
Some day you might stand on this spot, astonished
that twenty years have gone by.
You stare out the window
at strip malls, fast food joints, car dealers,
as if nothing out of the ordinary
could happen this afternoon.
Your mind's travelling so quickly
you don't have time to explain:
soccer moves, black holes, arpeggios.
Ahead, the tipping flight
of a turkey vulture,
tightrope walker,
searching for anything
the road has to offer.

August Nocturne

At this time of day
I move from room to room
pulling blinds, switching on lamps.

It's not the dark
but the slow drain of light
I can't bear,
the way things become half seen
before they disappear:
the dinner dishes on the counter
littered with bones and rinds.
The muddy running shoes
with ragged tongues, discarded
at the door, losing their edges.

Tonight some invisible hand holds me
fastens the gathers of dusk,
the only merciful delivery
into night.

Shadow forgives everything—
as fond of the careless
leavings
as of white
throats of lilies.

Domestica

I.
You sit by the window,
watch the moon spill citrus
over the strait.
I chop green onions,
pour another glass of wine,
turn up the Spanish guitars.
Jungles clamour within me—the song
of beating wings and cicada,
hot afternoons and nights,
snakes and revolution,
days so overgrown I can't remember
how we reached this opening:
flamenco and a yellow moon,
your face suspended in glass.

II.
I set the table:
a blue plate, a fine glass,
my mother's cutlery,
silver-plated with a flowery swirl
I'd never have chosen.
Fork on the left,
knife and spoon on the right,
the way she taught me.
Our hands
can tear and tine and cradle
but it's the same every night—
we sit across from each other.
You face the room,
I face the window,
both of us delicately armed.

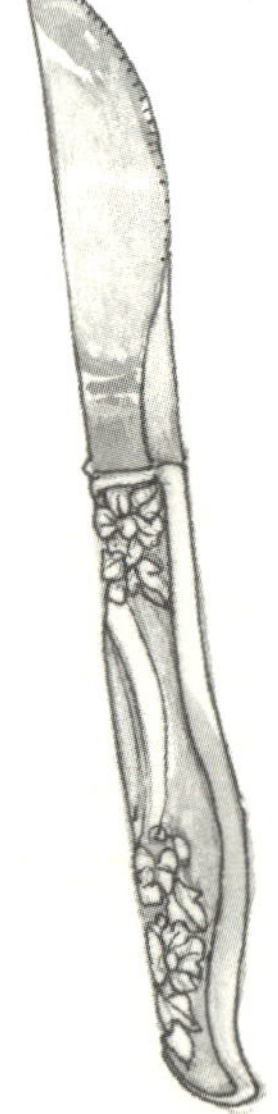

Japanese Glass Fishing Float

If
we had chosen a different walk that day;

I had been staring at the horizon
like you, thinking of flight;

I had glanced back at the carved whale skull
where hunters on the point once waited beside canoes;

You hadn't crouched
to pick among claws and spines for shells;

I hadn't turned to see you
from a distance, small, without armour;

the thought hadn't stopped me:
a rogue wave could lift us
break us apart—

Something fragile could have spun for years
un-shattered.

Garden Notes

I.
All spring she works,
bent, oblivious.
The soil she peels back
is thin.
On resinous afternoons she's a girl
standing in her father's garden in Santiago
before doors were broken down in the night,
before people began to disappear.

When there's nothing left to expose
she shovels dirt through a sieve.
Stones clatter, shaping dusty piles.

In shallow cracks
she cultivates only what's free:
cuttings, seeds that blow in.

II.
He moves slowly.
Emphysema bends his spine,
pushes his breast into a keel.
He's drowning but he can smell pale petals
opening frozen air. His December garden
has become enormous, a kingdom
he takes hours to cross,
each plant painstakingly
examined: spotted throat, winged seed.

The new year holds its breath, passes carefully
from snowdrop to witch hazel to hellebore
until it breaks into blood red,
purple, the hot spring yellows
of his neighbours' gardens.

He sits inside
smoking, waiting
for summer to end,
for the first buds
of winter.

III.
No annuals—
instant, shallow beauty.
You're pretending
you're never leaving this place.

You plant only the slow,
those that take years to flower.

And lost causes,
roses which curl with black spot,
buddleia spindly in shade.

Your habits have become essential
like a tree bending for light
long after the forest has come down around it.

A childhood of moving every few years.
It's just a matter of time before you abandon
the cherry that flowers mid-winter, you'll recall
the blossoms bowing under snow.

You plant as if you simply desire
autumn crocus, winter jasmine,
the weeping beech leaves'
pleated hearts. Deep down
as you plant you know
you will remember each opening,
thumb this almanac of loss
when you leave.

Protection Island Main

In rooms above us
the children dream,
milk teeth vanished
from under their pillows.

This winter night is black
as the coal tunnels beneath us,
stretching a mile out to sea.

They say at five hundred feet down
you hear your own breath;
the vein is so narrow
men work lying down.

Even the young ones,
returned to the earth
in small graves no one visits.

I close my eyes.
In the dark seam of sleep
bones become lighter,
hair turns grey.

To my Daughter, on Visiting Her Grandmother

At the hospice, I kill time,
flip through National Geographic—
Triassic, Jurassic, the Cambrian explosion—
while we wait to see Pauline Marie.

Once she was something
with her Chanel suits and cigarette holder,
her *je ne regrette rien.*
She'll be buried by a Catholic priest.

Shells, wings, bones.
There's comfort in these pages,
the way they're casting an essential past:
of course there were false starts,
extinctions, fruitless branchings,
but also: survivors.

You've inherited Pauline's slender legs,
her certain style. Your green eyes
you got from your other grandmother,
whose ashes we sowed together on the point.

We never speak of my death,
but for the record—
I'd sink to the bottom of an inland sea,
gather slow layers of sediment,
become stone, irrefutable
proof.

Recurring Dreams

I. We Move Again

Each house exactly as I remember:
the screen doors,
the kitchens, the stairs
to where I sleep
across the hall from my brothers.

The dark shafts
of laundry chutes drop three storeys.
Bedrock pushes
into crawl spaces.

But of how we lived,
nothing:
the games we played and how
we were different
with each move.

Did my mother turn grey
on Hart Street?
Was it the garage on Pine
where I smoked my first cigarette?

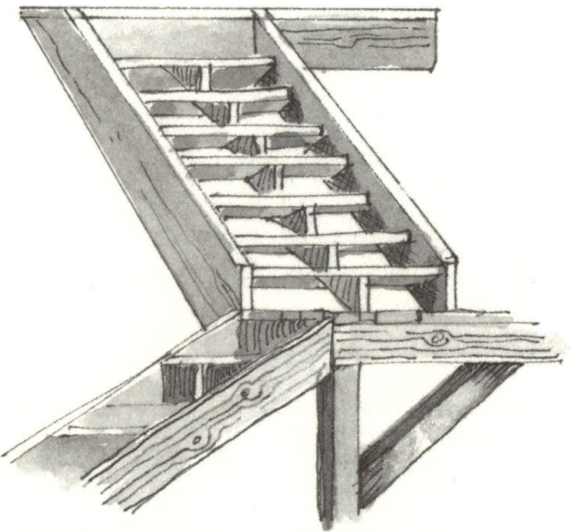

Was it there
my father stopped coming home?

In dreams
there are passages under construction,
open rafters,
stairways hanging in space.

II. You leave

night after night:
among strangers
at a New Year's party, break the news,
or at the checkout in the grocery store,
after I've searched for you down every aisle.

Last night you found me
at the top of a tall brick house.
I knew before you opened the door
that your face would lock
against my pleading. My tears
are wasted—there is another woman.

I wake
crying out, roll towards you.

In the morning I'm the only one
who mentions dreams;
love ends
the same way it begins—
mysteriously,
overnight.

Green Line

for my mother

On the Greyhound
in the front seat
so I can see the road ahead.

> I don't remember the arrivals,
> only leaving
>
> the first time
> with all my possessions
> in three boxes
> and later, at airports
>
> we hugged each other hard
> and sometimes,
> when I was crossing countries
> or oceans, you cried.

Two a.m.—
the passengers sleep.
The babies are quiet
on their mothers' laps.

Our headlights beyond
the wide shield
open the highway's dark unwinding vein.

The sky is needled with stars.

Last week in the hospital
I watched for hours
the heart line on the screen
for what it could tell me
about leaving.

From your face
retreating, nothing
to carry with me
on this night road home.

Cold Snap

Stuff the door cracks with towels,
wrap the water pipes.

The leaden days trailing Christmas forecast the usual
affective disorder.

Longed for hours of solitude whittle down to loneliness
while dark-cowled juncos rifle the feeder mix.

Fruitless season, neither an end nor a beginning
but a caesura through which the sad slip away.

Pick through your thoughts—
black sunflowers.

January 1st

We wake to the radio's usual retrospectives,
the year's first troubles.

Turn over— the morning is stone-cold,
jaded with rain.

We should make resolutions:
sort the family photos, write to the pope.

But the house is a quarry of yesterday's plates,
pits, peels, shells and bones.

By late afternoon daylight's thin rations,
eight hours, seventeen minutes are gone.

Now they're announcing: soon there won't be
room on earth for all of us to live this way.

9:21 p.m. we lose power. Darkness flares,
suddenly re-occupying night.

The sky clears. We could set up the telescope—
scan the report from spotless planets.

Sweetheart, every winter gets longer,
the news gets worse.

Come, the anchorman's fallen silent,
lay the fire, let's make light.

Anniversary in the City

Take a simple recipe of light:
mix spring, summer, fall, winter,
repeat and repeat
and repeat. Stir
and stir with your first touch,
the births of two children,
two-hundred and sixty full moons.

And we wake in this room on the thirty-fifth floor
to find we've been hauled through heaven so many times
it all begins to run together.

Give me time
I'll remember
the weekend the tide washed up to the flap of our leaky tent,
the night we lay out in the field watching for falling stars.

Every year gravity pulls us closer to the earth.

Give me steel, a glass
of something strong.

Give me your hand,
this dizzying view.

The Distance

The Shock

It was late September
when my grandmother got word
her husband was lost.

Somewhere on the great circle route
out of Vancouver,
his ship riding deep
foundered in deserted shipping lanes.

She was a new bride,
pregnant and impossibly far
from home, it was

sawmills and smoke stacks,
a wall of forest at the end of every street.

It was three weeks of waiting.

She was packed
for the train back to Halifax
when the telegram arrived.
Picked up in lifeboat one hundred miles off San Francisco.
    On my way home.

It was the shock
that marked the baby. Left my father
with the need to disappear over and over,
always drifting back.

Mining Town

In that town
men pushed the forest back
without looking it in the face.
Women taught the children
to repeat carefully:
never
fall asleep in the snow,
never play on spring ice.
Never walk into the bush.

But the children strayed
to the edge of town,
slipped beneath the forest's skin
flushing blackbirds,
red wings beating like startled hearts.

They bellied over rock,
peeling lichen from the claw-marks
of ice that once crawled there.

In that town
men beat brimstone from the earth
and women stitched the cold with small comforts.
The children,
sulphur-coloured bruises blooming on their knees,
scrambled above the mine,
swung from ore cars, letting go
in the moment just before
the ground below dropped away.

Six Deaf Girls

At night, when our leaders were asleep,
they tapped like birds on our cabin window,
led us to the still lake
in our flannel nighties,
called to one another with their long white arms
and slipped naked into the water.

At the campfire
they took turns touching the guitars,
their fingers plucking air.
They sat with their arms around each others' waists,
stroking each others hair,
watching the words fly from our lips:
He's got the whole world in his hands.

Birch Bark Letter

Father sent me a letter
from survey camp in northern Ontario.

It was written on bark
stripped from a pale sapling.

I don't remember what he promised.
Something that gave me hope—
he would return
before winter extinguished
the birches' yellow flames.

I remember the bark was fragrant as sandalwood,
and the way it curled,
longing for the shape of its slender trunk
no matter how many months I pressed it
between two books beneath my bed.

The Winter Before the Divorce

December drugged the fish
in the stoppered lake.
At the rink
eyelashes froze, mittens stiffened.

In January even the jays fell silent,
as if calls would shatter at 35 below.
My sister and I limped home,
lay on our beds, legs up the wall
to ease the burn of thawing feet.

Only the river escaped.
All winter we heard it
whenever we pressed our muffled ears against its ice,
murmuring in its dim corridor.

Leaving Foleyet

When we leave for good
there's no gesture of farewell.
The clotted grass still bent
beneath unmelting snow.
No bird ravels a thread of song
among the blackened flutes
of fireblown spruce.

My brothers run from car to car.
My sisters and I sit with our mother
on the red velour seats.

She never looks back
to watch the rails stitch closed the miles.

Soon the earth will rise,
fold the long years away.

In Vancouver
there's no sign of welcome—
only a tissue of spring rain
falling on cherry trees,
the platform a carpet
of ruined blossoms.

Winter Still Life

In my studio:
white paper,
a jar of bare branches,
rose hips. Rosa nutkana—

the wild rose
which grew in the lanes
of your home town.

I see you
before the bad marriages,
the smoker's cough.
A fine-boned girl
with straight chestnut hair.
One hand wrestles torn voile—
one of your mother's old skirts—
free from thorns.

Outside the window
snow melts as soon as it lands.
I pick up my pencil and begin to draw.
I won't look away.

The buds are corseted,
pressed close
against wine-coloured stems.

Useful Objects for the Afterlife

Last night I dreamed you were searching my kitchen cupboards.

This morning,
the story in the paper of a woman,
unearthed in a Siberian tomb
under twelve feet of rock —
curled as if in sleep. Scattered
around: combs, jugs, a cup
placed beside her mouth,
empty for twenty-seven centuries.

You never talk to me.
Maybe the dead are bored by the endless
chores of the living: dental care,
telephone calls, predictable
sex, Sunday dinners.

Maybe they're mad
we forgot to leave them something.
Think of the smallpox graveyard at K'san,
piled high with enamel bowls and sewing machines.

Perhaps what you need is simple evidence:
your bifocals, that tea cup
we bought in Chinatown,
your half empty bottle of *L'Air du Temps*.

Last Visit

I've never noticed how small he is. *I'm five and my father opens a battered case smelling of leather oil and silver polish. The sound of his pipes fills the house.* He makes coffee, moving slowly on swollen ankles, picks up his chanter and begins "Seaforth's Lament." *I'm ten and lying awake at 2:00 a.m. while he practices pibrochs at the kitchen table.* He tells me pipe tunes were taught from memory, sung from man to boy. *I'm fifteen and tired of hearing this again, simply trying to find a way to leave.* Remember, he says, the pibroch begins with a simple melody. His lungs are weak, but his hands are strong. *I'm listening to my father play, his fingers releasing grace notes faster and faster until I can no longer follow.*

Spring Chores

Sweep ashes from grate.
        (There will be no more fires.)

Clear gutters: leave nothing.
        (Fallen leaves, my father's death.)

Wash salt from seaside windows.
        (No mourning can withstand this light.)

Open doors.
        (The wind will blow through the house.)

Turn soil.
        (Nothing can grow that doesn't feed on what's buried.)

Make no lists.

Remember everything.

Circadia

Where to Begin

In this room, with its rough-cut cedar beams
I might contemplate
where they grew, the sun and rain,
and I would think
of those educational displays,
cross-sections of heart-wood
rings neatly labelled—
The birth of Christ, the invention of the steam engine—
and marvel at how each of us passes
only briefly through the life of a cedar tree.
But that's not exactly what I want to say.
There are other things in this room, the fridge
for instance, shuddering in the corner.
Here I could turn to that summer
when the babies were small
and we lived in a rental with an ancient turquoise freezer
I punctured accidentally with a knife
and stood by as CFCs hissed out.
But this would bring me
to how even the sky is precarious.
So I might begin with the antique sewing machine
stashed under the table, a Singer
that sews in one direction only. I could tell you
about the girl who spent days sewing skirts and blouses,
but I would have to talk about the mother
who taught the girl to sew,
and how I never erased her last message
on the answering machine.
What I really want to write about
is something reassuring,
say, the sea, beyond the window.
But then I think of swimming,
how the water opens for us when we arrive,
makes a perfect cast of our body,
closes seamlessly when we leave.

Vancouver Island Phone Book

1. Ahousat to Youbou,
you wouldn't know
every town's carved out of second growth
scarred with logging roads;
cities in-between—
Campbell River, Duncan, Nanaimo—
stink of pulp.

2. Everything alphabetical.
The Billies and Joes, no mention
of their Salish names, erased
by missionaries;
the displaced
Krezonskis and Yims,
who came to work in the mills.
No faded photos of the old country.

3. The tourist town where I grew up—
no details of how we lived
in the white pages. The boys
leaning on parked cars, Pink Floyd cranked up.
The girls spreading baby oil on each others' backs.

4. Nothing of what's disappeared:
a forest, a father, a maiden name.

5. Already out of date,
headed for recyling.

Skiing — Diamond Head

Each crystal type—
columns, needles, stellar plates—
how snow reveals
the architecture of air.

Where cornice is shed from black rock
to scarred chutes into avalanche fans
I stop and feel the muffled beat of fear.

I live by the sea now,
cross it every day in my small boat,
but this is the drowning that frightens me most—
the moment when the white slab beneath me suddenly tears
and I begin to slide,

the instant before it sinters like stone
and the glaciers hang like angels,
their terrible wings
cracked and blue against the range.

Journey to Earth

Wilson W. Bentley, world famous for his thousands of photographs of snowflakes, died this morning about 3:30, after a brief illness with pneumonia. He was 66 years old. He was a bachelor and kept house alone for more than 20 years.

—Free Press and Times, Burlington, Vermont. Dec. 2, 1931

At midnight
in the room where he was born
catching flake after flake
on a black velvet card.
He lifts them with a straw,
moves them with a jay feather
to his camera lens.

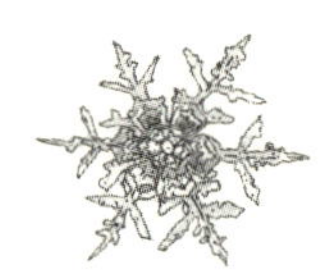

Scrolls, columns, filigrees of ice
spin above exhausted fields of sleep,
dissolve beneath his eyelids
when he wakes.

The storm has buried the moon,
ploughed the night into white furrows.
On the wall beside his bed
the barometer is slowly rising,
the blizzard begun.

If he had the strength
he would open the window,
the small, cold, six-fingered hands
on his face; he would see them one last time
and understand
what draws the frozen breath of clouds
into skeletons of stars.
Who can trace how the journey to earth
sculpts the solitary details of each heart?

The Invention of Birds
(after a painting by Remedios Varo)

All I know of the world
from this stone room
is a window of mute sky.
For centuries the stars
have been scratching at the dark glass.
It was the moon,
its slow hatching,
which I finally knew.

I sit with my threads and needles,
fingers stitch feather to wing,
carve bone hollow as flute,
start the minute machinery of heart.

In the morning I blow breath into song,
name waterthrush, honeycreeper, nuthatch,
at sunset, owl and nightjar.

I open the window. These others will escape
gravity, the tyranny that holds me here.

But a price will be exacted:
an invisible death,
a fugitive life.

Found Poem

(account of a dream, from an essay by German scientist Erwin Bunning, pioneer in the field of biological clocks)

Tropical midnight,
the full moon high above the zenith.
In front of me
a field of soybeans, the leaves
not sunken
in the night position.
How shall these plants know
that this is not a long day?
They had better hide themselves
from the moon
if they want to flower.

Berlin, 1934

At 3 a.m.
there is no reminder of the day:
cries, marching boots on cobblestone.

Erwin Bunning descends stairs
into the deeper dark,
the question burning,
how does a bean plant measure time?

Blindly he feels for the pots,
thinks of the men
who have fled— the ones
he knew at the academy,
diviners of atoms.

He has no mind for abstractions,
knows the secret life
of living things.
He tests the soil for moisture,
gently waters each plant,
listens for the scratching of needles
on blackened drums, slowly turning,
recording the rise and fall
of petioles: each night
exactly the same. He climbs the stairs.

Creekwalker

On the Canoona River
I meet a man who walks this path each fall.
See how the river
gives the Pink a hump,
he says,
the Chum a snout of snaggle teeth.

He opens a waterproof notebook.
Numbers must be fed: how many fish
have escaped the mouth and the net.

The banks are littered with salmon
dragged from spawning beds,
eye sockets hollowed by ravens,
heads opened, brains licked out
by the bears' hot tongues.

He lives alone on a boat,
a creekwalker for thirty years.

We stand together in the rain
watching the water, no talk

of hunger, exhaustion,
death and birth. How a river
changes a man.

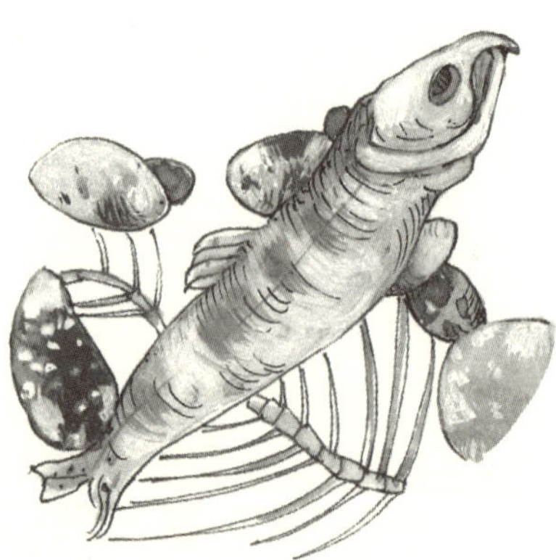

Key

1. If it is sunny when you read this poem, go to 3.
2. If it is raining when you read this poem, go to 4.

3. If you worry about the melting of the polar ice caps, go to 5.
4. If you're afraid you will outlast your teeth, go to 6.

5. If any of your ancestors knew how to use a sextant, go to 7.
6. If you've worn a kilt, go to 8.

7. If you're puzzled by God's persistent silence, go to 9.
8. If you've had a flying dream in the last month, go to 10.

9. If you've experienced *jamais vu*, go to 11.
10. If you've never had insomnia, go to 12.

11. If you can name five shades of blue, go to 13.
12. If you've taken ballroom dancing, go to 14.

13. If you've had shingles, go to 15.
14. If you've bought bird-flavoured toothpaste for your cat, go to 16.

15. If you secretly want to learn to play the accordion, go to 17.
16. If you've been to Kapuskasing, go to 18.

17. If you've used waterless car wash, go to 19.
18. If you recall the words to "My Way," go to 20.

19. If you know the atomic number of Carbon, go to 21.
20. If you believe you know why we're here, go to 22.

21. It will rain.
22. The sun will shine.

The Painter Considers Blue

FRENCH ULTRAMARINE

A woman leans
to sweep the fallen petals.
Soon it will be too hot to work.
Already the sun is so high
shadow has begun to fall
under the bougainvillea—
a precipitation
of blue holding
out against white light.

This is the place
in the painting where nothing blooms
or is alive
except the feral cat
curled against the courtyard wall
waiting for dusk.

CERULEAN

The high blue of sky
sifting down to horizon
loses concentration.

It's not simply a matter of fading,
but a straying
from conviction
until, balanced on the farthest hills,
the colour of doubt—a choice
you wish you'd made long ago,
something important
you've forgotten.

COBALT

Look as long as you want,
you'll see no ghosts
in cloud.

If you argue the case for heaven
it will neither nod nor disagree.
If you weep over an empty universe
it will neither dismiss nor comfort you.

This is mineral mind,
the colour of thoughtlessness—
what's always been here,
what will be left.

PRUSSIAN

Only on a clear day
in December
is this colour the sea.

The painter
feels the cold
through the old single panes
of her studio,
knows this bitterness
is best taken straight.
She erases the girl
standing on the shore,
the man rowing
a red-hulled boat,
empties the water
of spinnakers and gulls,
mixes blue
with the faint aftertaste of green.

Tango

The man in the magazine photo
stands on a dance floor in Buenos Aires.

He's dark haired
(grey at the temples as you would be now).

The only picture I have of you I took on a jungle trail,
in the moment you turned to look back over your shoulder.

The man in the magazine dances every weekend in a milonga
on the street where you grew up.

His hands hang loose by his sides; one knee is bent,
his head slightly inclined as if he's waiting or listening

to the singer: *I know that life is but an exhalation,*
that twenty years are but an instant.

In my picture you are underexposed, but
what I remember is there: hands of a mason, face of a Jesuit.

The woman dancing with the man leans forward on her toes,
forehead resting on his, arms flung out behind her.

I was in it for the heat, the thrill of heading deep
into forest, almost letting go of everything I knew.

There's no way for the woman to move, she can't go back
until the man lifts his arms, takes her weight.

In the end I lost my nerve,
left you standing motionless on a runway.

Names for Rain

Summers, it was always
the old man snoring.
My mother sent us out in slickers and gumboots,
we stamped through puddles
stained with gasoline.
Rain, rain go to Spain.

There were no words
for October's late rain turned to flakes even as it fell,
or the first drops in spring to collect
in cups of melting snow.

What about neon rain,
as I ran through the streets of Chinatown with my lover?
(Oh, I was over the rainbow
in those days.)

And what of the rain
that could not exhaust itself
for months after my son was born?

What to call the rain
that drenched me on the sidelines
in the years of cats and dogs
and games in the park?
The rain that dimmed
my mother's window
as she slid away;
that soaked the piper who played the lament;
that drips all night
from the downspout.

Letter from Jasper

The first flakes have begun to fall,
in the mornings
the ground scrawled
with elk trails and lichens,
apostrophes of seed.

Tomorrow it will be unreadable.
Another buried day.

Remember our first trip
to these mountains?
We skied to the backcountry cabin,
got so cold we thought we might die.
We kept the fire going all night,
huddled close in our down.

So much lost time
outside my window—
Edith Cavell tilting plates
of seabed at the sky.

Stone remembers
the hard parts of things.
Everything else—
feather, track, breath—
is forgotten.

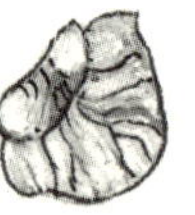

Kingdom of Chlorophyll

Tambopata

I. DARKNESS FALLS AT THE SAME TIME EVERY DAY

For you it will still be light and I worry
I've flown the wrong way this spring.

Twelve hours from Vancouver to Lima.
Below me the Pacific flyway with its lines of geese
heading opposite.

There's no spring here,
no theologies of resurrection,
simply dark and light.

If my bones were hollow,
if I could know the poles,
the electromagnetic lines strung between us
would be unbearable.

When I lie back, when I close my eyes
I feel my heart,
lodestone,
swing heavily north.

II. RESEARCH PROJECT

I don't tell the others
I'm losing my desire.

Each day when I walk into the trees
I drop another key
to kingdom phylum class order family genus species.

Insects hum like high voltage wires.
Birds rustle through leaves.
The forest plays a million instruments to itself
insinuating
taxonomy is dead.

On my back on the damp earth looking up
at canopy liana fern orchid moss lichen blossom seed—
kingdom of chlorophyll.

III. UNDERSTORY

On the muddy trail
shattered bowls of red petals,
a scattering of yellow feathers.
David's happy here,
dressed in camouflage,
draped with cords and microphones.
Light sifts a thousand leaves,
it's always dim, fragrant
with the hidden industries of soil.
You can't know the birds—
foliage-gleaners, woodhaunters, antshrikes—
without learning their songs.

He stops, sets the parabolic reflector,
records the wren's extravagant notes.
The bird is the size of a human heart,
cryptic in its dark habitat.

David's mind can't hold all this music—
he turns the silver disc skillfully.
Home to Colorado, he'll play them over and over
sitting alone while the first snow falls.

IV. MESTIZO

In the morning Luis shows me where to look
for jacamars and trogons.

At noon
I beg for shade.
We lean back
between buttressed roots.

In my dictionary I find heat, light, birds.
If I say them I will own them:
calor, luz, aves.

He tells me his father was a hummingbird
who visited many flowers, left him
with twenty-seven siblings.

I read *mestizo — mixed blood.*
Illiterate, he watches for movement, listens,
brushes the sweat
from the back of my neck with his hand,
speaking of other things.

V. NIGHT COLLECTING

Your letters avoid
expressions like "desperately miss."
You stick to your impossible hours
and how spring has infested
our apartment with palsied crane flies.

Here, the entomologists have arrived
pale in khaki and canvas hats.
In the afternoon they disappear into the forest
with nets and collecting jars,
return at night to hang a long sheet
in the field.

I follow them,
staring, blinded
by the white cloth
in the flood lights.

Beating against the sheet
a storm of wings:
glassy, iridescent,
lichened, owl-eyed, scalloped, frayed.

The entomologists say
most of these have never been described.

I can't sleep
deafened by cicada song.

I write to you
in the candlelight,
in a halo of a thousand
un-named things.

Light Will Get Inside Us

I. SONG FOR PHOTOSYNTHESIS

Light will have its way.

While we deliberate over wave or particle
it blinds us, burns our skin, convinces us
of summer mornings
when we lay on our backs and looked up through
the apple tree,
thinking the important thing
was wind, with its talk of improvisation.

Light will get inside us.

Listen:
blossoms are composing fruit.

II. SONG FOR MEIOSIS

Secrets are exchanged
between strangers
tied into twenty-three knots
where no one can see them,
in an instant
before anyone can stop them
or wonder
if a tin ear should be combined with a golden voice,
or long
for the familiar
upper lip, small of the back.
No place for sentiment
in this dark cell—
nothing will ever be the same.

III. SONG FOR MITOSIS

The helix uncoils
and parts,
lays its precious twins
bare. In its red-walled room
spindles align, the court knits
furiously, preparing for division.

Six hundred million years
cannot assuage the paranoia
of the twisted dictator:

there will be no sleights of hand,
no slipping in the unexpected,
no tossing out flatworm genes.
Even in this human heart

replication
is the only form
of flattery.

IV. TRANSPIRATION

Ten weeks of drought.
Tonight, finally—
a downpour; the breath of slaked dust.

I can't say what we talked about
the night we met. But I remember
the party was driven indoors by a summer storm.

Rain
—exhausted immigrant—
—heading home—
slowly climbs xylem ladders
back into the sky.

I need the photos now
to recall your boyish face.

I see us that night,
standing at the open window,
watching the inevitable clearing,
oblivious.

V. POLLINATION

It’s easy to be fooled
by largesse, this reckless
shedding of pollen
like gold coins all over town.

Spikes, trumpets, bells, perfume, nectar.
Everything’s on the house.

We squander fortunes of light,
fill our glasses
long into the night,
making plans
as if we have years and years to spend
while bees sleep it off in windowless rooms
and the peonies calculate
anther and ovary.

We polish off the bottle,
stagger to bed.

Petals drop like a thief’s disguise.
Precise divisions begin: embryos
fold into seed coats
hard as stone.

VI. ABSCISSION

We take the trail under the trees,
talk about your new office, the island gossip.
I tell you Mary's husband just walked out
after thirty-eight years.

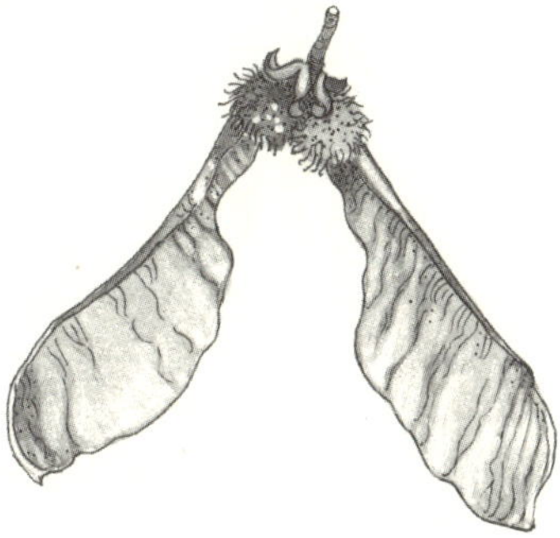

You don't remember
that it was this time of year
(the only time) I came close
to leaving.

In the crown of a maple
things change
so quickly: April's flowers
are fists of dry keys by October.

"Samara," I tell you,
the botanical name
for this fruit. Thousands litter the ground—
the necessary waste
to grow a single tree—
and stop to stuff my pockets.

Then I forget
until December,
when I wear that coat again
and wonder if it's too late
to sow them in the vacant lot next door.

In the end I put them on the kitchen table—
a bowl of tattered brown wings
once paired for flight,
each split with their single seed
along the invisible line.

VII. SCARIFICATION

The hottest summer on record.
My daughter comes home from Quebec
with a broken heart.

I make her tea
and sit with her on the couch.
In the red glare
of the TV news we see
forests consumed.

I could say
take fire, for example,
the way it prepares the ground.

In the interior
everything becomes kindling.
Towns are evacuated.

She goes to bed early,
sleeps late, stays
in her pyjamas till noon,
doesn't want to talk about it.

Imagine the lotus
after 2000 years,
scarred stone seed lying deep in mud,
willing to open.

Atheist's Prayer

Listen,
it's bad down here,
I mean hell-bent
tectonics, smart bombs,
floods and droughts.

It's not easy being godless.
First there was Darwin's
cold line of descent.
Chromosomes forever jockeying
for the next body ride down time.

Take a look
through Hubble's long stare into infinity
to imagine our loneliness.

I confess
I've found some comfort
among the diatoms and songbirds,
the mind-blowing beauty.
But this litany of extinctions
is too much. So ease up,
give us this day
without disasters.
Deliver us
from ourselves, hearts
scorched with grief,
forgive the way we can't bear
the thought of leaving.

The word CIRCADIAN comes from Latin: circa, "about" and dies, "day." It refers to the innate rhythm found in almost all plants and animals (expressed in everything from leaf movement to sleep cycles), which is about a day in length.

TAMBOPATA
A biological research station in Amazonian Peru.

LIGHT WILL GET INSIDE US
In photosynthesis, light energy is used to make sugars, which build plant matter (i.e. leaves, stems, flowers and fruit).

MEIOSIS is the process in which egg and sperm are created. A cell (which has two copies of each gene — one from the father, one from the mother) splits to create two cells with one copy of each gene. Before division, genes are exchanged between maternal and paternal chromosomes, creating a completely new mix of genes in each new cell.

MITOSIS is the process by which all other cells divide. First the chromosomal strands of DNA in the nucleus open and are doubled through perfect replication. When the cell divides, each new cell has a complete set of chromosomes and is identical.

In TRANSPIRATION, water that has travelled up the plant from the soil is lost to the atmosphere, as vapour, through the leaves.

ABSCISSION is the dropping of leaves, flowers, fruits, or other plant parts, usually along cellular lines of weakness (abscission lines).

SCARIFICATION is the etching and scarring some seeds require before germination. It is believed that scarification ensures that the seed has spent sufficient time dispersing away from the shade of the mother plant.

Acknowledgements

I would like to thank the following journals where some of these poems have appeared: *Arc*, *Backwater Review*, *Event*, *Prairie Fire*, *Room of One's Own*, and *subTerrain*. Other poems have been anthologized in *Vintage* 97-98 and 99, and the chapbooks *Poems from the Basement* and *The Invention of Birds* by Leaf Press.

Thanks to the Canada Council for the Arts for the financial assistance which made it possible for me to work on these poems. Also to the Banff Centre for providing the perfect writing retreat.

I am deeply grateful to the Nanaimo Poets for their compassion, support and for the careful attention they give to a poem.

Thanks to Patricia Young for early editing and encouragement.

I'd like to express my deep gratitude to Sue Wheeler, for her generous help in shaping these poems.

Finally, many thanks to Beth Follett, for her meticulous and sensitive editing.

SOPHIE WATERMAN

ALISON WATT

Alison Watt's first book *The Last Island, a Naturalist's Sojourn on Triangle Island*, was short-listed for two BC Book prizes and won the Edna Staebler Award for creative non-fiction. *Circadia* is her first book of poetry. In recent years she has won the *Backwater Review*'s Hinterland and *subTerrain*'s Lush Triumphant poetry contests and placed second in *Prairie Fire*'s competition. Alison Watt writes and paints in her studio on Protection Island, near Nanaimo, BC.